MY LOVE IS A DEAD

the shadow I make with my hands:

ARCTIC EXPLORER

two wolves kissing

AHSAHTA PRESS

BOISE, IDAHO

2012

THE NEW SERIES #46

MY LOVE IS
A DEAD
ARCTIC EXPLORER

PAIGE ACKERSON-KIELY

Ahsahta Press, Boise State University, Boise, Idaho 83725-1525
http://ahsahtapress.boisestate.edu
http://ahsahtapress.boisestate.edu/books/ackerson-kiely2/ackerson-kiely2.htm
Cover design by Quemadura
Book design by Janet Holmes
Printed in Canada

LIBRARY OF CONGRESS CATALOGING-IN-PUBLICATION DATA

Ackerson-Kiely, Paige, 1975-
My love is a dead arctic explorer / Paige Ackerson-Kiely.
p. cm. -- (The new series ; no. 46)
Includes bibliographical references and index.
Poems.
ISBN 978-1-934103-27-2 (pbk. : alk. paper) -- ISBN 1-934103-27-6 (pbk. : alk. paper)
I. Title.
PS3601.C56M93 2012
811'.6--DC23
2011043607

ACKNOWLEDGMENTS

Thanks to *LIT, Verse, Typo, Third Coast, Saltgrass, The Laurel Review, The Salon,* and other journals
where some of these poems first appeared.

"Cry Break" and "The Misery Trail" are available as broadsides from *Typo* and Rope-a-Dope,
respectively.

Several "This Landscape" poems were created in response to the work of artist Adie Russell, and were
originally published alongside her images in a limited edition art folio by Argos Books.

Thank you to the following people and organizations for supporting me during the creation of this
book—Family: Christopher Kiely, Saskia Ackerson-Kiely, Tinder Kiely, Theimann Ackerson, Suzanne
McMurphy, Keil Ackerson, Nancy Bacon and Peter Bacon. Friends and neighbors: Karla Van Vliet,
Karin Gottshall, Michael Chorney, Rux Martin, Cheryl Brownell, Matt Schlein, Piper Westbrook,
Cynthia Bystrak, Allison Titus, Janaka Stucky, Sarah Goldstein, and DJ Dolack. Gratitude also ex-
tended toward The Willowell Foundation, Jentel Artist Residency, Vermont Arts Council, Ahsahta
Press and Janet Holmes. Special thanks to Joshua Harmon for introducing me to Byrd's work.

CONTENTS

"Even in my most exalted moods I
never quite lost the feeling of being
poised over an undetermined footing,
like a man negotiating a precipice who
pauses to admire the sunset, but takes
care where he places his feet."

ADMIRAL RICHARD E. BYRD

THIS LANDSCAPE OF REQUEST

Imported meadow. Noon-pled
thunderheads darkening.

Had I a shadow to cease
this squinting. Scenester

of compelling location—
I would make you come to.

Taken by forest. Implored
riverbed to all-over-me lave.

Demanded deer nuzzling
a pile of trash. Had the refuse

been important enough: No deer.
Bid you come out of the tool shed.

Had I a parlor, a pellet stove, were it warm
enough without tampering. Could I

sit still. Petitioned reciprocation
of my hands on your face

in any of the above landscapes.
Called for gentleness,

the somniferous monogamy of grass
brushing the ankle, sky above bleeding

blue. Were I to quit this angling,
this remittance. Appeal to the pocket

of your overcoat that my hands
might fill. Had we a home.

Had I ever been pleased.

DRIVEN ALL THIS WAY

Driven all this way, the dust behind the car choiring up in brief staccato, the clip swift enough so that every home appeared as a starched white sheet tucked around a woman's body: The breasts two roof peaks softly letting snow and the calf to the upturned foot a breezeway leading to the garage. I was lulled, cowish, by seemingly limitless cud. Driven all this way, to the laundry in the laundry room, I deconstruct the unaroused sea, towel by towel. There will be no comfort at the beach today. Driven all this way, through the declarative traffic lights: I just want you to stop right now. Past the great limitations of love plainly announced on the elementary school billboard: Early Release. Driven with care to the stocked refrigerator, the journey from death down the throat in one quick swallow that the tilapia's sacrifice might save us. Driven to choke back, to unquestion—driven, shakily, to contextualize the enemy in every imaginable sphere. Driven to make the best out of it, as if best were merely unfocused acquisition, a flabby pile pushed in front of the door to prevent quick entry. I read your book and I could die anywhere.

THE GREETING

It was the middle of the day. Some neighborhood kids were playing in the sprinkler. I stood watching them, though I wanted inside, a room benighted by eaves, thrum of the fridge dimpled by an occasional loss of electricity. Transient-fault. The town flatlining just long enough so that grief and hope are momentarily confused. A stranger walked slowly past my house. *Man's feelings are always purest and most glowing in the hour of greeting and farewell.* All that jazz, I never got into it, unless someone was watching. He was, so I snapped my fingers. Can you dig it? I am no gardener carefully tending this plot of bored declension. The kids left, sprinkler still whizzing glee. Deaf puddles flayed my yard. The stranger paused to look at me, then beyond me toward the neighborhood kids out back, huddled under a quilt printed with old French country scenes. An older boy pulled down his pants in that dark den. I do not recall the face or name, just the parasol that opened in my gut. Hello, I ventured. Hello, I strained. His face imparted negligible vehemence, a soggy bun slapped with meat. For some time, the only thing I could recognize was my own hunger.

HAVE NEVER BEEN A LONELY GOD

I have never been a lonely god but can relate
to inventing warm bodies
shuffling across plains shuffling
flush me, lay me out upon thine table
I only wanted to present my hand—

I took his business card.

It read:

A life alone makes the need for external demonstration almost disappear.

It read:

The most likely explanation is that the trouble lies within you.

As a girl I leapt toward a
quantity of din, the amassed
leonine snarl captive in the
cistern of the throat. The
starkness of the card table,
emptied. I called a hundred
times. My voice broke into
many people I would like
someday to meet.

We met as in a deck, two planks fastened
    to hold, as in a deck shuffled upon one another.

Courting through walking, each leg
frantic for the brush flush against the
other leg. My pants were not quite right.
We walked. He pointed to a teetering
cairn, and I knew I was a teetering cairn.
He led me to a dark room and turned
on a little light and I knew as though I
had always known: I am a little light in
a dark room.

I have never been a lonely god
though I can relate to being asked for many things
& fighting the urge to give them away
just to get him to shut up.

You must be gentle sweet girl

You must not fight the buttonhole, you
must touch the waistband put your dukes
away touch your hair for what seems like
an hour touch your ankles your ankles
with their bony mountains & the old songs
mountain people sang as they ascended.

                    *

I imagined I was a soupspoon, I was a ladle, a multitude
of tines tipped with halibut, a sheathed knife though
I wasn't safety. I was no helmet law.
I imagined I was a head injury, a contusion of the most
brilliant crimson, crouching beneath the temple
waiting for the temple to open.

                    *

He led me to the store.

You can have anything you want.

The economy faltered, I omitted myself
from the widescreen version where the economy played
a more comely me. Never again to be
philandered by a dress, never again the smocking
at the bust, the pleats undulating pristinely
satisfied to be remaking, anew, the failing of the body.

*

I wanted to be his eye, looking at me—
shivering tensile—the back, shivering: *Throw something over me*
  throw yourself over me easily
as the only survivor of a plane crash, an infant
buried in his mother's arms.

A gamble always to remove your clothes or go anywhere at all.

In Texas Hold'em the two players to the left of the dealer are the small blind & big blind, respectively:

I have never been a lonely god
but when he kissed my mouth
I could relate to the creation of a varied terrain
like Braille under my foot
I cannot say for sure where this is going.

I have never been a lonely god
but I understand the way rocks
just lie there waiting to be formed into tools.

NATIVITY

A native of small towns shuffling towards obsolescence. Of
The Waffle House, undelineated slop filling the belly, child
my child, of uniform holding, the way the window frame
just keeps the glass in place ignorant of view, child my child,
we are native. Of gas stations we are native to the buzz—the
deep inhale crouched over the nozzle, killing the receivers
we are native to, having received so much & piling it into the
closet to be guarded warily. My child of the act, we are native
to years undoing the late night pawing—desperate dog at the
door—clothes cast over chairs & all the dishes in the world
undone, ready to be beckoned forth. My child, your creation
undeserved; like backing into a van in the parking lot. Both
vehicles totaled to nothing worthy. A native of your crash,
my child, & your stare as if from a box of food teetering on
the precipice, starvelings gathered round. A native to this
dirge of gray mountains, your hand feeling along the granite
boulders, *why here & how to make it defensible,* your hand
pushed deep in your pocket as a doleful rampart holding you
upright, your hand tossing down smooth white stones, that
you shall lead us home—

FIRST CONTACT

Name this:

The sheen of his face
like the underside of grounded leaves.

She is getting up from her chair,
wiping crumbs from her lap—

To lie down. *Let me speak*. To lie down finally
she has cleaned herself. He has erased the feeling
a child has about dog-earing books: Everything is
smooth & everyone remembers his place. *No,
let me speak*. She enters his room—

The guy who got famous for writing that girls
very long ago were innocent, & sad
because they were innocent, & beautiful
because they were sad, is dead.
She is all full up with his nightstand.
His little lamp makes her sick—
Turn it off, turn it off!
Let me speak. Her body if after heavy snow
pushed into banks, his face,
the gravel imbedded.

Name this:

If you buy shoes
from a factory where children work
so many hours then go blind then die
you have agreed that those children should
go blind & die? She like a whisker
measures each object in relation to her body:

He is mostly in the other room
unknotting his laces. LET ME SPEAK.
The wall is too close to her back.
How almost nothing happens
in the middle of a bedroom.

Snow from the television—
the kind that strong men give up inside of.

Storms arguing over a factory if only
for a moment, the sound is that of teeth
being poured from a pillowcase over a tin roof.

First snow of a Vietnamese refugee in Duluth.

First snow a passel of dresses
in a large wooden washbasin churned by oar.

First snow the way one reads it a second time,
for meaning. There is nothing to see here.

Please, let me speak. First snow the blanket
pulled up to her chin. First snow his hands
felt cold even when summer came.

ARS POETICA

The stairs led to a hallway. If there were rooms, they were
appointed with an ordinary candor that didn't really beckon
or repel, so I stayed in the hallway and looked upon them
as one might a tonsil, depressing. The sheets lay flat upon
the beds. Not once had they been tied to a bedpost, let from
a window and carefully slid down until a foot touched the
grass below. All grass is a relative of the poet Donald Justice.
In fact, I cannot think of grass without imagining how it
goes yellow secretly, and at the root. It was maybe a Tuesday.
Fat flies concussed lazily against the windowpanes. A baby
cried out somewhere—its mother brimmed with resentment
because she just wanted one hour, one single hour to admire
the desolation of the torn couch and the browning banana
that stared at her, alone and uncircumcised, from the fruit
bowl. Of course she'll fetch the baby; she's heard about that
instinct from a variety of sources. Donald Justice said: *Let
summer come with its schoolboy trumpets and fountains.* There
is no stopping it once it is outside of you, even if you wish
your love for it were dead, and its jarring wail that eulogizes
you night after night were dead, and that you had no name.
I spent the entire day gazing into those rooms, pressing my
forehead against the cool wooden trim of the door. I could not
utter my secrets. I was angry at whoever invented the color
taupe. I did not know what time it was, the clocks were sad
and stuck. If I could draw a picture of what was inside of me:
A doe breathing in a meadow.

THIS LANDSCAPE OF FOREST

Where I lived for many years. Boardinghouse of flocked nightgowns, sunless girls wrapping locks of hair around rags. Took my first tipple there, a ritual that came to replace vesperal ablutions, replace the bedside lowering, soften the mind to near love. Learned the difference between clown and mime was not silence, but skill. Ran my hands along a wall of my invention, was often climbing imagined stairs, spent hours picking invisible orchids. Sometimes I was a man coming on to me. Shy in repose, I rebuffed the evening shadow as a boreal conifer feathering out, cast my fingers across the door draft to pluck a most dolorous credo. No one listened, even those who looked. Once, in recalcitrant vignette, I posed for years as a girl who didn't know a goddamn thing, my homeland was a single shaft of light across floorboards, the dust shone as snow in a Pasternak diorama. This is what I remember every night as I emigrate to your border. You are sitting at the computer, maybe paying bills. Your dark limbs laden with my favorite birds. Their happy song I am trying to make my way toward.

BOOK ABOUT A CANDLE
BURNING IN A SHED

One time in a shed a candle burned.

My thoughts were with the window
looking out over the dark yard.

I know it isn't much—
the light inside just strong enough
to illuminate nothing really out there.

I snuffed it. The shed continued to contain me.

If you toss a penny on the ground eventually
the ground will gather the penny into itself:

No imagined bank for saving poor white girls
on the sawdust-covered floor where he

traced his finger under the waistband so lovely
I paid him back by keeping still.

MY LOVE IS A DEAD ARCTIC EXPLORER

Waiting for his love to take, I held him clumsily. His face was without form and darkness moved upon it. I was told: *You must keep him still for six days.* I needed to be sure he did not try to leave, so I asked: *Let there be light,* and the sanatorium became light and it was a soft yellow light, and good to his features. He was thirsty on the second day so I said: *Let there be water apart from the earth,* and a glass of water appeared at his bedside, and it was good clean water and he drank it as though its existence were not a miracle. He drank it like he was impartial to dying a general death. He drank as if I were not watching him, imagining how someday I would let him go, and it was good, good he didn't know I was already dreaming of my solitary reinvention. On day three he became hungry and agitated so I begged *let there be grasses bearing seed and also some fruit from a tree as sensuous as a woman he imagines when he enters me,* and thus a peach became visible and I fed him, and all in all it was a pretty good show. On the afternoon of the fourth day the beasts were called, creeping things that frightened me and fowl and cattle beneath the window of the sanatorium, grazing passively, grazing on really good grass. Day five he coughed like a badger clawing a warren where I hid, hedging my bets, living in my fur as I was granted control over all of the beasts and thus fashioned myself something warm and attractive from the rabbit. And it was good, looking good, even though I was afraid.   He called out some names on the sixth morning. He said *barstool* and *dispatch* and *megawatt*

and *Thermopolis*, and all of these things became as he called
them and it was good, it was good to have a list. Later that
evening, after he described *fortitude* and *unctuous* he said a
word I had not heard before but it made my teeth ache and
a slow itch spread down my forearm and I thought I felt a
dainty woman wearing one of those fuzzy pastel sweaters
with a plunging neckline standing close to me—her soft
breath against my neck—and I wanted to kiss someone really
bad but also to remain still forever so that this feeling might
be known to anyone who happened upon me. He said *Helper*
and he made a motion with his hands, like he was breaking
an egg onto a hot frying pan while a hissing sound emerged
from his mouth, after which he lay back on his bed with his
arms thrown across his chest like dirty laundry. Although I
knew not of dirty laundry at the time, I understood he was
naming me and it was good. It was good to place my head in
my very own hands, which were not as I imagined them—
hatch batten downers, Pious, wincing shovels—but as he
named them: Your *Hands*. And with this knowledge I rested.
I dreamt sweetly.

You've been conjuring her every night for as long as you can remember. Always she is wearing the same dark blue dress with a Chelsea collar and pearl buttons ending at a drop-yoke waist. Always she removes her matinee gloves when you ask her to take a seat at the kitchen table, the stove throwing off slumber-heat, dishes undoing themselves with magisterial shyness in the sink. On bad days you notice her lips are shaped like the very pocketbook of collusion. She rummages the rubbish bin, eats the note beginning: DEAR BELOVED. It hurts to look at her but you get used to it. On good days, the veil of her smothers your ordinary body, she licks your ear, her decibel just short of roar, and you know starvation is the only choice for her chaste containment. Never consummation—your fantasy—this invention of wooing. Every night, for as long as I can remember, I've gone to bed hungry. Always without you. Always the stark white sheets turned down in glacial tableau, flashlight aimed at the wall, the shadow I make with my hands: Two wolves kissing.

AND IF

And if there was light:

And if there was a pitcher by the bedside:

And if there was a shudder in the flank of a
racehorse
who must sit this round out, who has but one
single job to do in this world & cannot do unto
this job: If there was a horse called in
to the barracks, brushed out & tied to a post.

And if there was light:

To say I love you. Then to say his name.

And if there was a pitcher by the bedside:

To ration the water. A horse has no gall bladder
but breeds as though trying on a dress at the mall.
The struggle to fit. To be rained upon—
if there was a shudder in the flank that gave away
nothing: Then to say his name.

And if there was light:

His Scarboroughed muzzle. The bit. Each night a little
more action at the local bar. The neon signs

less abrupt under the cool haze that shows the flaw
to be immaterial. Drunk & recollected drunkenly,
a horse out to pasture—all hours of the night
are foundered, all poems contain the words
Terminal Daybreak—the horse knows
what the horse is spooked by.

And if there was a pitcher by the bedside:

To maybe raise the thing up. Floodlights
in the basement of the chest. Silence like the
potato of the sternum, de-eyed. Running in a broad
daylight. Running & running
until finally asked to stop.

THE DOG

To try at loving in the town—
the crepuscular men slouching,
to try at loving the men
in the town bent fetal around the church.

Say the clock strikes. You are in the park.
In the park you are
many men striking out
on your own. It is the first time
you have felt like hitting an animal
& the first time you have understood
why an animal retreats to its cage.

The sun of the sternum & the ray of the rib.
So much prismed laughter.
To really try at love in the town;
to just go on good faith that a dog will return
if you let it out
& go to bed without the dog.
To tell yourself to go to bed.
To tell yourself to close your eyes

or call his name all night. The option of
prayer all twisty-tied. The bread gets
moldy in its see-through dress—
call to him one last time.

The bread in the cupboard inedible now.
Potatoes bolt in the shed.

Say the clock strikes. Several days
since you have seen him in the park
you notice a hole in the ground
& you know you are a hole in the ground
but you don't know who made it.

To tell yourself to go to bed.
To touch the dog, to thrust your fingers
in his mouth. Say the clock strikes.
Say the clock has struck. It is wicked late.
You are searching the park for your name.
You are excited to answer.

GIRL NEXT DOOR

Tired of the doorframe's belligerent threshold, the idea of a meadow 20 paces away as counterpoint to the dishes, that we do and have done, generatively let's add, like a smoker inserting gum before a kiss. Tired of the kiss, of reclaiming the kiss, the eyes hugged by lids unpainted, not resembling the blue hue reminiscent of orgasm, the flood of blood to the lips, the nag of the lengthening neck. You've pictured it while sweeping, you've pictured it when buying corn from the farm stand. Even your children, may they rely on other streams, have been saturated with your ordinary water that pours quickly into containers and rots the root. It's so pathetic, starving after the pulpit—allowing a secret blush you hotly amidst the same old proclamations, like car-pooling as a remedy for carbon footprint. Forget binding, the stub of his longing you hobbled after. Forget the car idling in your driveway, you may leave only when you are ready to leave. Let morning come without the pornography of the kettle, its catcall of pick-me-up, the yard of dandelions, all of their faces lifted, all of your faces lifted—to the sun. Now, think about blindness. Try to make your bed.

GOOD MEN

Having only ever loved
Good Men, dark brows
furrowed over
their faces' gentle slope—

you expect the mountain
of it to wind you,
your breath
another rapid thing
to collect
even in descent,
especially when you slip,
alone & probably bleeding,
disoriented. Having only
loved Good Men

isolation becomes default.
Like how you look sort of mean
when you aren't trying to look nice—

Good Men! Especially those
from the North Country.
How you love the North Country!
Scrap heaps, mud, the way people
never scream. Knowing someone
with a terrible secret,

guessing at its source,
again & again—

you love Good Men, the North Country,
the Source—!
Foxes spray a dead birch,
fiddleheads adjudicate the lawn.
Getting turned on in the car,
heat cranked: Don't forget
the brickyards, Good Men

shuffling home after close.
It isn't as lousy as it sounds:
It takes nerve
to do the same thing
each day, & to
not kill yourself.
All those bricks! Enough
to bury a body
under no
body, sometimes
nobody at all. Years in fact.

THIS LANDSCAPE OF COLTISH RECPROCITY/*OCEAN*

Out of the glovebox comes whatever snack a passenger can hand you when you're driving. So many years spent distilling head-nods, the occasional small wave off a steering wheel, brushing against a stranger in the dairy aisle, her heat and yours. Sometimes, fleeting eye contact with a wild bird, or loving a workingman without interrupting him. It has been difficult. A jetty quelling breakers; punching someone in the face then blowing on your fist. It has been difficult. Your $\frac{3}{4}$ ths coverage, the remainder of me shrugging away. All the trinkets I gave to you hidden in your dark desk. I always retreat when I come right up to the edge, like this second-to-last line. Though I love the way it feels like drowning, your mouth against my legs, moving up.

SMALL DETAILS THAT COULD NOT BE GLOSSED OVER

Your hair was the wheat filling thousands of Vodka bottles,
that I might drink.

Your arm the shirked tree limb in the orchard, covered with
   apples,
that I might mend.

The sheep in the field, imitating each other.
Loading docks smothered in brown boxes.

Everything is plain, my love,
is ordinary.

Let's see how this goes:

I'm walking out into the meadow.
I understand grass, am not afraid.

The small stand of trees defending shade,
that I might watch over someone as radically.

And Lo, when I cannot lower over you
I go to the bar, my love, where

the wild beasts approach. Your paws I
once conjured as indifferent—

I am surprised,
that I might hurt.

Everyone watching me die on that barstool;
all the bottles on the shelf, all those secret recipes.

What you are looking at when you look
at a woman, and she's not that pretty.

The way one leaves before last call
to avoid the indignity of being reminded.

PROVISIONS

The party is winding down. You are alone in the bedroom, listening to Shirley Horn. Her voice is the body of an old woman, stripped, standing relaxed before you: What can you look forward to. Someone in the other room wonders aloud: *Where are the coats stashed?* This is another cue you must learn to pick up: At a certain point one makes a definitive journey, it begins with a simple request for provisions. *They are tossed in a pile on Matt's bed.* You are allowing Shirley Horn to think for you. You notice one heavy wool coat is sprawled atop the rest—he is the only coat that can breathe, the others suffocated, his arms feeling up their plackets, his chest pressed lengthwise into their waists. You are humming along to Shirley Horn, feeling for her under the coats. He feels you back, grinding against your arm, animated by a sudden gust of wind from the cracked window. You didn't ask for any of this. Night unmaking the garlands of small talk you practiced, petulant curtains occasionally slapping your face. You reach into his pocket. For a five-spot you'll put him out of his misery, push him from the third story window to the street below. He pays a handsome tip. You button him up, give him a shove— but the remaining coats are just as lifeless as before. It's too late, as usual. Shirley Horn's final note is a moth with a drop of rain on one wing. If you don't kill the moth first, it will eat through every beautiful thing you own. You call out: *Does anyone have a shoe and a tissue? Does anyone have a shotgun, a bottle of pills, a match?* No one answers. You sit down on the bed, wondering how you'll ever leave.

DON'T TREAD ON ME

To all the middle school kids slumped over milkshakes after screwing up lines in *You're a Good Man Charlie Brown* in the All-Nite Diners of New England. To their mothers chain-smoking Camel Lights, and to the phones—preyed upon for the messages those mothers might extract as a gold tooth from the enemy's mouth. To the patch of grass at the edge of the diner, dead but unburied in hoary November—and to every November, which is like waiting for a man to shut off the light and make his way to your body in the way one searches the bottom of a pool for a nickel. To your body, soft and sopping, to your body the shame of the sheets that will have to be wrung-out, and to the sheets twisted like a loosening noose around your abdomen. To your abdomen—a bowl of baby eels shocking their brothers—and to the brothers in Supermax, no strangers to shock. To Supermax, ADX Florence, called The Flourishing after a man named because of his crude delivery from his mother's abdomen. To the opaque nature of the disposable milkshake cup, which hides true knowledge of the amount slurped. To the body that will digest true knowledge—to the body where hunger resurfaces like a late-breaking wave in a birdbath, to the hunger that was given over to math worksheets and vocab lists, to the hunger that was urged to hustle and thus kicked a ball into the wrong goal, to the hunger that blew pot smoke into the dog's face, to the hunger that left you too weak to ask for the right things. Stand up now and salute yourself for trying.

PRESERVATION OF A LOVE

I assumed that I would go to Greenland
and nothing would be green.

The position I assumed was that of a bowl
brought by a Dane to Greenland,

along with wilted lettuce—as with most dying things
I have been writing this poem

since we met. I love you, Greenland,
a man who will lie with a tourist as two hands

that have never met—one knows to keep
still around a weapon the other holds.

I'm certain there is a method to peace.

But no schooner slinks up
Champlain to the Saint Lawrence headwaters.

I cannot get where I need to go despite
Vollmann's myopic account bearing
the loveliness of sludge weighting the Black Robe's hem:

So I slowly turn, and in so doing kill the Indians,
what for, kill the bare ground throughout Autumn,

traipse it infertile until I am Greenland, spit
in the greater ocean, drowning, colonized mouth—

glad you are frozen inside of me.

A SONG

I need you to pick him up by 6, then drop him off for his 7 PM lesson. You'll have to find something to do for that hour. You'll have to wait in the car, vessel imbued with no spirit; you'll have to read a magazine, if that's all you thought to bring. It is October, you must allow the car to cool slowly, do you understand you are his mother. Wait for manhood's encroaching visor, your son's soon shielded eyes, not by your hands, no, no longer. There is too much not to see. It might help to picture the piano teacher, *soft touch, pianissimo,* she instructs—your son, whose music still sounds of the toy car he drove across the expanse of your abdomen. Headlong off the cliff of your pelvis. The accident is ordinary, he walks away, nary a scratch. He walks away; you try to look casual, reading your magazine in the dimming light. You think you hear him singing from the open window, a low, baleful note a lamb might make from its well-tended stall, even though it is warm and has enough to eat. The failure at gratitude the most common of sad sounds. Later, you recognize the voice as belonging to the local meteorologist, coming from the radio of another parked car. It will be a cold winter. You try to imagine how dark his hair will grow.

LETTER OF EXPLANATION
TO MY DEAD ARCTIC EXPLORER

To love the other side of the sea. To capitulate that which was not allowed into my life this time, I have forgone the boots, years passed, the anorak became snug and the pull of the night seemed immature. OH PURIFYING DARKNESS I called out, oh the need to go unseen and the special powers when held aloft the notion that no one really wanted me. Naked I set out, one lousy foot in front of the other, and I could hear the great left spiral of the narwhal twisting, and the glaciers twisting then falling, then falling to my knees. It is out of exhaustion that we lean-to other people, our own bodies crooking gallantly as we debride a keepsake from our lover. It is not a lock of hair. It is not a lock of hair. I took him everywhere with me, some boreal ship plundering was I, some faux-gulaged countess counting him in all of the one-man sleeping bags, the limes, the 12 long feet of walrus, the zeroing of the stars as they consume themselves thoughtlessly. I took him everywhere with me, I wasted his time with my factoried abstractions, I cheapened him with warehouse beauty, applied the products in hasty strokes with supplicating hands, I killed him slowly with my lonely sex—I grieve for everywhere but right here.

NOTES FOR A DAUGHTER
LEARNING TO SWIM

You've seen her entire body. Her amazing legs, for example,
the gunwale of her thigh, where someone could walk
cautiously to the cabin. In tumult, a smart man on hands
and knees, keening to himself, mouth to salted plank—he
means everything when afraid. But she's upright, moving in
knots, baptized nine years ago for the Dutch. You decide to
see your entire body. It's not pretty in the mirror, but you've
told a different lie. How you landed here, Pitcairned. The
law will keep you from certain things: Throw her asunder. In
time, someone will board her for a fortnight. *Don't be afraid,*
daughter, you want to say. Bilge water everywhere, especially
in the throat. It stinks like fish at certain times, but you get
used to it. A good teacher knows when to keep quiet. And like
that, you want everything you've built to silently sink. The
price for loving her so much, as you do, you would extract
from another by way of Beardman Jugs filled with brackish
water. But we're reporting on a different story: She's dangling
a foot off the dock. It's so lovely outside. *Careful,* you say. The
best things in life are impossible. The best things in life never
even happen. She plugs her nose and dives in. She surfaces,
waves to you from a short distance. She's laughing.

THIS LANDSCAPE OF SKY

You bent over everything.

You were as the neck of every coat hanger, a Tyrolienne tune missing the low back quadrant of the throat, the bucket of pig's blood in Carrie, fingers raised in quotation gesture for emphasis.

You had mothers upon mothers languishing on shabby couches so high up in your mind you appeared as an orphan.

Danger-green, gangrene, dropping limbs on icicled paths, negligeed sylph adjudicating importunate syllabi.

I wanted to be beckoned into the picture, just a little handshake, to follow silence into fallow violence, proctorial elegance heavened from one apologetic utterance; a deer under your great robe.

You bent over everything:

Your sun skirmishing, clouds—grave balloons heralding deluge. If I continue this dance will the rains not come?

THE PITTANCE

On my pittance of *I'll do you if you do me,* I have been strict in my stillness. It is a matter of indecent accrual, stacked upon, a compost of googolplex that the world should be mine for this pale, shivery packaging. If you love me I will love you back. Spoiled dogs do not strain forward out of love, but for continued spoilage: Eventually you end up at a destination derived from the cartographer's immeasurable desire for one true proportion. His cold-cracked hands lifting a camisole of cloud, sky behind mocking the bar's neon invitation to drink a specific drink. Though we felt the same long night thirst, while those dogs worked so hard I continued to whip them.

MISERY TRAIL

I spied eleven lank deer in one evening
feeding on different lots.

I thought a lot of those
whose kindness like a string on a balloon
held me aloft over numerous grasses
but never a grass unforgettable.

And never in the river the same water over a rock.
To be lonely like your own hand. To be so
goddamn lonely with just a little information.

I spied a telephone ringing the distance
between one stalk of corn and another.
At certain times of day a field can blind you.

So I walked, uncharacteristically slow.
You couldn't know how slow I walked.

THE ONE-LIFE THEORY

Good God take your long cold look
like they do in the moving pictures.

I was a study in ash,
so lightly I breathed & the candle was
snuffed.

The thought of your hands is holding a bird
& snipping the tip of its beak with a nail clipper.

The thought of your hands on me
is eating what is clipped. The acolyte's hair
in his eyes.

I must, dear Lord, in your robes upon robes
I move my hands in & out as though they are curtains
and you are one big day,

I must bring to my lips the hush of you
silent because you are looking so close

as I studied, Christ almighty, I bent over
as a woman knows well to-do—
harangued, coat-hanged, I looked

so beautifully down for a while
the trash on the ground was my friend.

CRY BREAK

The day the news rolled in that half of the world's population had perished via an anticipated but still shocking chemical explosion, even the Country Music Station recanted on its promise: "All Country All The Time." Death on a large scale always takes precedence and allows one to act swiftly and without guilt. I kissed my brother-in-law at my mother-in-law's funeral, the ill-fitted plank of his torso hewn to my grief, so that afterward it was easier to be around the happy stuff everyone seemed to remember. It was all very confusing, as the radio put it, "complete mayhem." I thought about going to the school early to pick up my daughter, but decided against it—all those children parroting sorrow, what did they know? Sure, a few of them had been slapped, spit upon, held down and raked over—some had been told the truth: YOU WON'T GO FAR, YOU WON'T GO ANYWHERE AT ALL. I love my daughter, the pale gloaming of her hair a minor song of my continuance. Unlike the Country Music Station, the day the news rolled in that half of the world's population had perished, I did my chores as usual, putting the dirty clothes into the washer and removing the clean ones from the dryer as if the world could be soothed by the delicate cycle and the loving heat of my steady machine. It was as though I knew I was not going anywhere until an anticipated but still shocking chemical explosion allowed me to perish from my daughter, my swift, guiltless death an event that would bring context to her sorrow and allow her to remember, unbidden, the happy stuff, which I'm sure happened daily, like writing your name in the fog on the shower door, for example. I thought of the way the singers that particular station favored created a chest-pulse, commonly known as the cry-break in Country Music, and how I had, while doing the laundry or tending that which required my tenderness, until that moment, been really listening for it.

PROMETHEAN DILETTANTE

I was a Promethean dilettante
disabused of tinder.

For one match to strike against
the heavy black canvas of his coat

I waited in a long rain—
Ipswiched in rural Mass,

great father winking;
a lighthouse on a foggy shore.

Wanting to be the one who loves
everything the most. Fine crackle

and spark. After you reach adulthood
no one bets you'll set this world

on fire. Sodden hair I would have
killed to sweep from his face,

great father, would have killed
to give myself over to your careful

pyre, calico aprons yellowing
in a pit where we would lie together.

This is all I can think about.
All I know I guess.

I wanted to love the glowing tip
of a match shook out. I thought

to be extinguished by his quick,
merciful pinch. Great father between

your thumb and index finger and you
would not touch me not once

cool my turned cheek ablaze.

THE METEORITE

Robert Peary was such a jackass to the Inuit people—do I have to be explicit? Robert Peary is the source of every blood stained mattress dragged into the woods and forgotten. When a woman has alopecia we call it Robert Peary. When a woman has alopecia and must be examined on a mattress in the woods by a doctor who does not wear gloves, Mr. Peary was behind that arrangement. Need I continue? Primary contact with Robert Peary is an endless arctic night. Secondary contact is an endless arctic night that is also insane. Have you seen a night go insane? Imagine that we are finally together. I am drawing my finger under the waistband of your pants. Then a black vapor leaches out of my eyes and everything I gaze upon shrivels and dies. Don't make a joke about how it is a good thing I haven't gotten your pants off yet because this vapor also kills everything I rest my mind on. This is how a night goes insane. It is brutal and you will surely die even though you are strong and beautiful and I love you so much. There is no way around it. I used to be a jackass to strangers, just brushing past them on my way to the market to buy bottled water and limes—but those strangers were not being discovered, and if they had a meteorite in their backyard from which they chiseled tools important to their survival, I did not know of it. I did not help myself.

MEEK OVERCOMING THE MEEK

I do not know why you have to go so far away to explore when there are plenty of things around here that need sussing out. Just today I was contemplating over a sink of dishes my unrealized dream to become a tightrope walker. I understand for you there is a notion of velocity, the percussive abuse of a foot which falls continuously and without regard to physics. I get your mastery of weather, that you will have to whip back at the wind so that the wind will doldrumize an expectation for death that may hasten you back, into my arms, into my arms which enable me to hold you but also clean out the peanut butter jar and put it in the recycling bin. Imagine what it might be like to be strung up in the amphitheater, a crowd of breath-holders secretly rooting for your plunge, while you step, gingerly, a distance of approximately 120 feet, only to be diminished by an applause which is its own abrupt weather. I am asking you to consider for a moment the woman in the crowd standing next to her boy—she covers his eyes until you have completed your routine, your sermon of the meek overcoming the meek so that we might be able to have a real conversation instead of inheriting the earth then holing-up on private property. She is wearing a dark blue shirtdress with a small pattern of roses on the sleeves. Her son stands absolutely still and rises to her shoulder. In two years time he will overtake her completely. In two years time they will find him locked in a utility closet at the middle school, holding a rifle across his chest like those long poles amateur tightrope walkers use to reduce angular velocity.

How I want to tell you this boy's name, but the papers won't release it, intent this nation is on protecting the identity of youth. I want to deliver a call from the porch that reenacts so many nights his mother announced plainly: *Time to come home! Come home!* To be suspended above that mild evening scene, him ditching his bike in the bushes and racing up the steps, her clapping the flour from her hands in small bursting clouds before she embraces him, smells the top of his head, leads him inside and closes the door.

SOME REASONS FOR THE WOODS

More than knotweed, or the trammeled
stylings of Karen Dalton—

(how hard it is to tell
who's gonna love you the best)

More than a dissonant thrum of bored fingertips
on some immaculate surface beating out:
Shut-up-and-move-on-with-it—

Or vegetal reliquaries bound in soil absent of prestige;
throwing away the contents of a fridge—

In spite of the hopeful looks of children
forming a straight line at the door
the appearance of gratitude
and resignation difficult to delineate,

like the border in Northern Maine—
thicketed wasteland limped across in hopes of finitude,

not the getting-shot-at kind, but the end
of such vastness—More than that, even.

The trees, lo, the trees. More than their cowering
hair, the ruthless angle of their
bodies poised skyward—

How they bend over you with what appears like concern.
Like most Americans, you approach everything
with an unexpressed need for consolation.

It isn't a crime to walk into the smudge
of forest asking, *have you ever felt?*
No.
The trees do not think you are crazy.
The trees do not consider you at all.

BIRTHDAY

It was when I said: *I don't want a goddamn thing from you,* and then, under my breath, *or anyone else,* before storming out, that the scales began to chart my decline. It was the 12,775th lie I had told, one for each day of my life. Brittle leaves curled and chattered beneath my work boots—the sky was monolithic, sacrosanct, the kind of thing you knew better than to mess with, and I walked below it to a small clearing in the woods. I could see, just over the ridgeline, the remnant of a chimney's warm vernacular, I could smell the lip-gloss I applied an hour earlier, and while facts such as these, when confronted, often induce me to skim, I must own up to them now, omission being another crime for which I was in grave trouble. I sat upon a rock. I will not describe it, not because I am withholding information about its character—grey, lichen-streaked, cold as a day-old bath—but because I am not certain that it wasn't a stump covered by the tarp that blew off the woodpile. In my mind it stands as a rock, and as I do not have a sketch of myself leaning in forlorn attitude against its felsic table, you will have to take me at my word. I sat there for about 10 minutes, considering how best to enable good graces once more, for I could feel my head beginning to throb, and an unusual crick upon flexing my wrist. I set about to create the list of things I didn't want from you, a list that would surely reverse my deterioration, make plain once and for all the truth of my singularity. As the list grew, my decline did not abate, for the lies I expelled or backed up were merely compressing more lies, intricate, wound round as a bolt of black lace. As such, my hair shone silver, fingers took on the crook and gnarl of an apple tree, my ears rang with tuneless bells. Recall slowed, the list slowly slowed, and I became aware of one or two things: I did not want to keep the baby, this was already on the list, but I wanted you to want me to keep the baby, and I wanted to keep the baby for you. I wanted not to keep the baby, but if you did, to name her something serious, like Dolores, with its the root of pain and grief, which, I suddenly recognized with a fair amount of surprise, was exactly the name of what we already had between us. With this knowledge, I arose from the rock, limped inside, my heart snarling indiscriminately against the chest's delicate fence. You looked up from whatever you were reading. My sight had dimmed; I could not see. *I'm sorry,* I stammered, before my head hit the floor. And then, so quickly, it was over.

WAITRESS ADDRESS

The body was a language and it talked to itself. The body was a chopstick, a kettle, a regrettable dishwasher holding the crystal to the light, saying, *not quite yet*. The restaurant was filthy. The manager touched her face in the bathroom as though it were a staff meeting, saying, *regarding absence please call, please try to get through at least twice;* the way a man has to wait at least an hour before having another go. The body waited for response. It grew tired proffering plate after plate bearing death that was inconsequential. The death on the plate absolutely silent as when they remove a man's hands, according to Shari'a—tossing one into a thicket awaiting a bird's manic touchdown, the other hand miles away, bagged and left in the hospital dumpster. Don't think it didn't hurt; they wanted so badly to speak! To raise the fork as though it were an explication, each tine an independent song, hither and thither to this, thine mouth. I did not understand the cutlery tray. I could not speak of the napkin's tremendous folds until I flattened them as a sheet sodden and afraid of being entered. I am ashamed, the great flock of cadavers lain out for dressing just so by my body. Hello. Who will breast the plates as such. Who will thigh the terrible sigh. I am waiting, dear god; I am actually speaking to you—

STATIONS

Instructed from a young age

not to touch:

What would they say to

your body, not a flame

rising in defiance over

the happy shingle

of my figure, but a gestating

smolder I birth long

over the valley—

the pitchy Pines death hum,

rabbits nestling

in the intricate warren?

Hey, I've felt something

for the stove's front burner.

I've lifted my arms over my head.

An unarmed woman

policed by platitude and

the occasional headlong glance.

I ran my hands over the entire world,

brought them to my mouth:

But you could not take me to the station.

ON AWAITING YOUR PERCEPTION OF
THE MEADOW

Did I not love the beast, the nostril of the beast, fanning out
as a woman's Easter dress. Did I not touch the pond and in
doing so the flagella, the tail of the tadpole, the sperm, did
I not barricade the sperm; *past this level of initial sadness
do not ascend*. Did I say no to the child, nononono no. Stay
where you are in your clean dream with a balloon affixed to
your delicate wrist. Did I not weep into my wrist, weep into
the wrist as though it were beige office furniture. Was I not
holding in my heart the sigh and the pink slip. I was wearing
the slip, the fabric atop wishing to cling as one would to the
edge of a crevasse. And the big damn holes, everywhere, I
stumbled, did I not, I fell as one falls into the word love,
as one falls into the particular face of a word that does not
smile, the mouth is a line, the mouth is a trolley straight to
the loading docks, workers heaving boxes, sky above failing
cheer. Did you not love me I did not ask. Have you never torn
into the earth, ripped up the saw grass as it imparts its honest
reach. Are you not inclined to create a ruin for the tourist.
Take me to the pasture I am waiting for a sign. As clouds
enphlegm the sky's vast lung, tie my hands and march me to
the highest knoll.

SEXTING

Go ahead and criticize our slick machines, photos of hands moving across so much hairless flesh, external organs preened to nest in a cool and ready palm. Say what you will about the way we treat the geezers with their gizzards no one would boil and strain for stock. Their clock's done broke, they wake at 5 AM, peering into empty academies. Just play along, act like they were too busy walking to school in a blizzard or pinched into feedsack dresses rendering suet over a dull flame to have time for such wont. The thing created out of duty lies dead on the factory floor, half dressed in bubble wrap, but don't think the paycheck doesn't come. We're born. Every Thursday night out at the bars. If Ma could see me now; if I punched a wall and the wall had eyes. No, it's not that simple. If it was simple to fix she'd be driving right now, plowing all relaxed through several states in the heart's covered wagon, eyes half-closed against the image of Pa tugging a razor across his throat. The thing created out of duty looks into the mirror, same time, different day. The thing created out of duty and all it got was this stupid t-shirt. If it was that simple, she'd take it off, drape it over one shoulder, like a sail slack in no wind, mast-straight back bedewed in gentle fog, while in the cabin below a man spits chaw into a tin cup, cooks his fish, remembers fondly how hard it struggled. Tell me this, who doesn't love a painting of a sailboat? Who does not want to be helped aboard, out, finally, of such impersonal cold?

NORTHERN FADO I

Finished with most sex
by thirty-five. We wanted
the old pastures back, cheaper
rates at the motel bordering
old pastures, at times
a distant train we recognized
simply as moving along.

We were tired of thinking
about school shootings—
we just wanted to lie down—
nipple of afternoon sun
lowering over our faces,
pulling back abruptly
as we made to touch it.

We practiced contentedness,
staring at that before us
until it broke down into
the story of a pane removed
from a window, propped
against a white-washed wall.
We understood the concept
of being fucked over
as a necessary component
to it being over,
over—

Sometimes, a petite woman
in an eyelet blouse reminded
us of our bodies.

We sat very still. We did not move
for hours. Eventually,
we forgot again.

MEMOIRS

As a major league baseball player for over 20 years I thought
I'd seen it all. If you want the details of what I saw, you can
buy my memoir. It's called: *Every Diamond has a Particular
Setting to Elucidate Its Beauty*. The title was as much in
reference to baseball as a nod to my wife. Though we were
becoming more or less estranged, it was of highest import that
I be acknowledged as training hard in the field of domestic
propriety, despite the overgrowth of silence between us, so
thick it could not be broached without a machete. The title
also served as a private reminder of my next enterprise: to
marry the woman I'd been sleeping with for the last 5 years.
It was lonely on the road. The telephone poles flashed past
the bus windows in rapid succession, it was helpful to think
they were trees. The woman was a skyscraper made of glass,
glowing coolly into late, industrious hours, her long arms like
empty elevator shafts you'd scale to the correct floor. She liked
to play games that had only one rule, a relief, really, after a
life spent in terminal adherence to the conflated inventions of
man. The night of my intended proposal, she instructed: *you
may do whatever you like. The one rule is that you must treat
me as though I am the last frog left on the planet*. It seemed
simple enough—a perfect cocktail to emulsify the tenderness
that filled me as a vernal pool teeming with the very protozoa
of frenzied desire. I drew a tepid bath, placed her in its
embrace. She was still, silent, as I touched her dorsolateral
derma plica, her breath-skin, the perfect teardrop of her
external nares. I chased her around the hotel, the slipstream

of her thigh eluding my grasp. Finally, I trapped her under the sink. *You're all alone,* I said, winded by the tempo of her game. *Your parents are dead. Your friends and neighbors, too,* I said, certain of this as any one thing. *Thank you,* she replied. *Thank you for understanding the one rule.* After she left I called my wife. No one picked up for what seemed like hours, though I was asleep before midnight.

THIS LANDSCAPE OF RETRACTILE LONGING/*ICE SHEET*

Lost him, and the petty things she hated began imitating her: pale bedclothes, pre-portioned vanilla sheet cakes, songs about wanting him back even though he treat you so mean, huh, people who aren't good-looking. First time she heard *It's a Man's Man's Man's World,* went white to realize she wasn't one whole thing. Sometimes Drunk for an entire weekend, listening to herself break up to bits over this terminal geography. Waiting for man to make the train, the kind for heavy loads that don't need describing if you've tried carrying one—it can't be slept off. Man made the boat for the water—of this she was most certain, though resented the comparison to Noah's ark, as she'd've rather gone extinct than carry on this bastard race: Baby girls and baby boys getting psyched for any distraction. Lost him, again—mostly drunk for a whole weekend, bobbing alone in the living room. Sometimes a reflection swayed back in the frosted window. *Welcome home from the wilderness!* she might slur. All the furniture pushed to the edges of the room, the floor a scuffed ocean. She stood resolutely in the center, as if she'd ever been lost.

ON THE FAILURE TO MAKE HOME

O highly stylized warming hut—
mats just lying down where they're
tossed, provisions pressed into
cabinets left open as a woman
paying off her passage
here
the problem's with not using
what you have.
Naturally the explorers left
their shabby parlors, purloined
wives bent over the gruel, the problem
with not asking for anything—
someone draws the curtains
now you just stare at the curtains.

PROJECTIONS OF THE DEATH
OF AN IMPORTANT FIGURE

She knew her father would die & hoped when he did it would come swiftly, with a purpose not unlike the way he often phoned her from the road: She would tell him her fear that she would not survive life as a young mother working in small-town retail with no real friends. He would not say that she would survive, nor would he attempt to build up her position beyond a Calvinist: *Do what you have to.* Before hanging up he always said: *I love you.* She would then go to sleep only to get up a couple of times during the night to let the dog out. When morning interrupted her for good, she always walked into the kitchen, which was oriented east, made some coffee, maybe turned up the radio & was comforted by the way Scott Simon always had something to carry on about, & felt both shame & satisfaction that her concerns were at least Middle Class. When he died it was an ordinary Tuesday in March. Her dog had produced a litter not two days prior. There was but one survivor. She took her dog & the now-starveling pup to the local animal hospital, a solemn double-wide with limited parking next to the High School she had often expressed reluctance about, on the phone, whenever there was dead-air or her father asked after the fate of his Grandchildren. The vet, with a face like a pink eraser chewed on during some unimportant exam, explained gently—but with aristocratic frankness—that some bitches are simply ill-equipped to care for their own.

ANORGASMIA

It's true I've always wanted to contain
the magnificent.

Evenings when the children
would not stop laughing
I dosed them with cough syrup.

The parlor with its rare
furniture and formal
mood: For you
I assemble this ceiling.

Some nights turning off
Jazz with George Thomas
to hear the low moan
of the refrigerator.
Don't forget: Some places are cold.

You know how if the ocean
spread blue over this valley,
that blue would just slay us?

I'm up for a week on the Cape with you,
but must remain onshore to build the levee.

Sometimes a bird sings in my chest.
I hold my breath. I squeeze your throat.

ARCHITECTURES

Everyone has their building
tall enough to jump from
      with predictable outcome.
Variegated wings plushing
the down draft. Everyone
in flight
       over everything.

Yes, you do.

Your building of shabby austerity—
peeling contact paper in the shower stalls,
      corridors scurried through,
silent empty medicine cabinet   maybe painted white.

There was pain on the first floor;
     there was pain on the second.

Everyone has their building;
Stalin had his building.

A wife on the third floor.

Pretty wife, laugh
that sounds like a weak engine
            revving. It does not catch, she does
not turn over.   Liar.   She does.
She goes up the stairs.   Pain on the fourth.

Yes, you do.

Live here. Quit knocking after month 14.
Some religious orders use a vow of silence
to gain the trust of others.   Greater Silence:

Even the lamb's bitter when shorn,
to make a blanket you might cozy
                        under. Not prepared to provide:
                Your clothes vast rags tied to a tree.
What does he want compelled
the tides, the dust on bookshelves.

Lesser Silence: Eco-phobic. Philtrum-deep.
Nary the tepid shallows of the bathtub
filled,   nor the sink dished upon lazily
could induce your slow rise from the couch.

Radio on.   Someone's dead.

        Pain on the floor, hurts like snow.

Soft at first.   *What does he want*

compelled the bread to mould, to turn green

& slick because it was not used in time.

Yes, you do.

Before the building,

       simple tree,   rappee'd bark,

       volant limbs, Matins-prepped.

That there was sun & gratitude.

No one rolled their eyes or pretended

to be waiting for someone else to show.

Erstwhile, garrigue a garrote snaking ever

up this informal tree party.   Sorry you didn't know him

                  for how he stood around

prescient back, stiffening bark.

You don't remember carving your name

         or your name loving another.

Yes, you do.

Pain in the hallway.   Pain
in the kitchen. In all the ghastly drawers.
Fixing supper for the children
        you didn't want to think of Tillie Olsen.

You're lonely he said
        & came on in.
This is not about bespoke suits
their cranberry linings
interspersed with grey thread, reflective
        like a gas-puddle, or anything
        inside of you hinted at.
The clothes do come off.

What is your mother's name   he asked.
        I became an orphan.
Your favorite animal
        Something eats me when I lay down.
Your sweet face
        Could not walk.   Never got me anywhere.

Yes, you do.

The building is an animal's belly, sliced.
You climb inside to get out of the cold.
Pain in the forest, men with flashlights
                            turning over wet rocks.

This isn't going well—
            wanting someone to love you
                    you don't want to love back.
                    Pain in the sky
bearded the sun. Pain purloined
in dull silver,   you counted your money.
You had five dollars.

Yes, you do.

For three years your husband's
cool back,   night-pled urgencies
turning on & off the lights.

Your children like bitter weeds
            growing into ward-off stance.

Pain on the deck where they played
pain on the ignorant deck where
they shot each other with fingers cocked.

He was there & not, like everything
that melts.   You were covered in his
snow.   Pain in the mudroom where your
boots leaked him out,   where he ruined the floor.

A long time ago
he was a boy,   in those days they let them be—
filthy, & embarrassed by his mother's call—
                    Won't you please come home you ask.
You didn't know him then.
            The door ajar, he brought bugs into the house
when he fell you washed the gravel
out of his knee   —you are just a girl—
the gravel,   tiny mountains bursting
from soft loam. Everything is red
& hot between you   & his pain,
            which is new to him every day
but for you has lost its originality.

If you squinted you saw covered wagons full of blonde
children.   In the parlor
they built a window seat for you.

       He is the age of your mother.   He listened
       to The Doors & did lines
              while driving.   Your bonnet was askance,
you looked down invitingly,   but not for him.
He is 7 years younger than
       Father mucking the stalls. You show him
the photos,   NICE he says,   & presses
you against the barn door.   Pain in the latch,
the hinges strain like something wants out.

Yes, you do.

       Presently, I'm afraid he mumbles.
His throat is wrapped in motel drapes.
There he is,   your baby,   but you can't
       take him home from the hospital
can't bring him to your breast while the orderlies
       tidy up. Pain in the Spackle, in the
ceaseless drywall dust tunneling the sinuses.
The nursery is never finished.   The nursery is boarded up.

You take him in the cellar. You take him
way deep out back in the shed
quickening every step. Your husband's
                    reluctant touch lashes the horses:
          Let's move this house, your husband says.

You take your baby to his wife.

If your five dollars could be broken into
thousandths for each wrung out sob. Buckets
of tangy metal.

He does not cry on his porch-step,
                    the basket of your chest
               full of withering fruit   & sure, it's
          for the best to throw it away.

Pain on the cutting board,   pain
          in the distinct twist of the sheets.
The way you might be shocked to find
no body   beneath. No smell of figs
          & mud. Pain in the still lips,
in the tectonic curtains smashed

together.   The same old continent of privacy.

The same old sea swallowing.

So you walk on home,   that's what you call it—

Yes, you do.

LAKE EFFECT

You're at the bar again, trawling. The net of your eye catches the man in a wheelchair, sitting next to you. Forget pity, it's for the full-bellied. Forget how the northern Lake conceals not only fish, but also trash, petty currents, your foot in the mud sinking lower. You: *Wanna go back to my place?* The Lake's shifting boundaries—you fight on no soil—probably, it's raining outside. *Yes*, he says, *your place*. Forget pity, it's for the one who's already run to the horizon, and is now looking out over the Lake, pleased to be alone. You drive him to the Lake, but his chair won't make it over the path. Forget carrying him. The Lake buoys the dead like terrible logs to the edge. There's an old, blue tarp in the van. You place him down, face-first, on top of it. *Hang-on,* you say, as you said earlier, the bass tugging imprecisely at your line. He hangs on. You pull him over roots and rocks to the shore. You flip him onto his back. *Can you see all right?* The Lake is impossibly clear: You trace the outline of his jaw. Craggy isthmus. *What's your name?* They called it after the first white man to explore it. *That's pretty.* You're a rivulet careening, feckless headwater charging the Lake. He's so calm at drowning. *There's Canada,* you point and whisper. Lazy America, content to proclaim: *You can't get there from here.* Forget America. You're unbuttoning his pants. Slipping off a dock. Feeling around for the bottom of it. You think you could make it to the other side, but have never really tested yourself. Clouds come softly. They come over the Lake sadly like hundreds of white mittens too big for your hands. Then they go away.

MAIN STREET

Say what you will about the skyscraper's
colloquial prowess: We already felt
tiny on our porch steps.

Forget the sarong or the coverlet—
the vast grove of oranges, an
empty tetherball court repeating itself.

You are an investment banker.
Who says adults no longer play?

That every blade of grass nonsense—
that place we put the people we promised
not to leave behind.

This is our confession. This
is how we had to kill ourselves—

when you say: No man
can hope to be
completely free
who lingers within reach
of familiar habits and urgencies.

Pity the gate we pry
open so weakly.

PASTORAL AGGREGATE

The whole of Vermont
is a romantic term
for a box of chalk.
I don't know what to write
to move you toward me
things are kind of coming—
You think I'm strange.
Afraid of some things:
When I was little,
the disembodied voice
at the drive-thru.
Father finding out
I had an abortion
& not having strong
feelings about it.
Either way,
knowing there is only one—
or pretending this will do:
Silver birch, milk-maid, fallow
deer making it through November.
How many beautiful women
spread naked on camera.
Trembling
in the last dry leaves.
It was never the first time
I laid it down. Familiar organ
music insinuates homesickness

or to look homesick
at least
I did not love you
because it was right.

GLOBAL WARMING

Maybe you are working in a convenience store making change for the newspaper when it happens. You are suddenly in love. Your arm extends to receive the cash as though the customer was helping you out of the bath, the bills like towels he might wrap snug around your waist, the chime that alerts you when the door opens, opens every noise inside of you. And every noise inside of you returns the one long noise of your love— let us say it sounds like a door closing over and over. The customers hear the door closing and become afraid. Those with watches check their watches (you kiss the inside of their wrists) and those wearing high heels bend over to make sure their heels haven't broken (you remove the shoe, you bathe the foot) and those with nothing grab a bag of peanuts and begin to study the ingredients list, which is short: PEANUTS, SALT, then they return the peanuts to the rack and continue to have nothing because there is no pretending. Don't be so afraid—look, you never had anything before, but now, suddenly, slam, it is love—unstoppable, sealing you in. The criminals searching for an easy target do not have a bag large enough to stuff your love into. It is the most valuable thing in the whole store. So when your drunk boyfriend picks you up late and spits in your face and calls you a whore, or your boss tells you he is cutting your hours so you sleep with him because there is not a bag large enough in which to stuff the reasons not to; it will be all right. The doors will close. Over and over. There isn't really anything else they can do—they are frighteningly automatic, after all. They keep the heat in. There is an energy crisis the world over.

NUMBERS ARE MANY, WORDS ARE LIMITED

How many times we did it.
How many nouns we can replace with it.

You say fulcrum; I say plinth.
We better call the calling off: Off.

Your special note cards full of sums.
What real estate is worth when you rent it out.

If my embarrassment raised up as a hair
on the hackles of a jackal. No—

if each jackal, crouched under this charming sun
could describe my ear, warmed
only by your swarthy breath—

as often as I could say:
I want you. Is never
enough.

THE GLACIER

What we had in mind was ascent. What we were thinking when we pictured it was how it is possible to take back the thing we did when no one was looking by securing distance from the thing and the ignorance of it. What we liked best was the way we appeared so small we could lie down and wait to be touched as a baby, and when touch did not arrive we could walk back to camp as adults, eat a biscuit, have whoever remained, and feel content, as mostly we cannot do. Our mouths tasted like a cormorant in flight over nothing, our tongues were the cormorant's heart, pulsing in rigid meter— though we did not speak—we could not speak the heart's jerky metaphor. To say: *I need to be alone in the ablation area, among the calving bergs,* released into a sea's vast plan to hear our own swimming—for once—above our own drowning.

REAL MOUNTAINS

You see a mountain on the Internet;
You go to the mountain.
On the Internet, you click on the mountain.
Rapacious pines tweed the hem
of the mountain. At the base you
have a husband & two children.
Some of them will do drugs.
Some of them will wake up
in the middle of the night knowing
that you did not ask for them,
but they will not ask you to confirm this.
Such is the nature of inquisition.
This mountain. Twenty thousand unique hits
at the peak. You cannot speak of the precise
depth at snowline, but through research can
present an average: Most black men will
not hurt you & most white women
will not sleep with you. You know
you are the lady who must get a drink first,
before mingling, but no one seems to notice:
Always you lumber crassly up the steep incline.
It is easier to admire people from a great
distance. You think your family should
be starting after you before too long.
This is not a question: This is a mountain.

THE END OF NATURE

You are pretty sure the end of nature has arrived. No longer do birds trill from the forsythia, for there are no birds, no forsythia, and the itch in the belly that caused you on some spring nights to dream ardently of your lover feeding you, one by one, the sweet petals of clover then slowly unbuttoning the deadness you perceived as terminal winter, ceased to dew the tender grass. Your mouth is a dry straw sucking wildly on air. And the air, you guessed it, is like the air in an airplane at cruising altitude, when you are finally allowed to unbuckle your seatbelt. Free to move about the cabin you seek out the restroom, because, as Rilke put it, a wedded couple is nothing if not guardians of one another's solitude. And though you are all alone, and on your way to Cleveland to learn something you already know about a job you hate and thought you would have left by now, you close yourself into that small compartment, noticing that the last resident forgot to hold the lever down on the toilet. *It's all a shit joke,* you think, and it is better that you don't share this with anyone, because Jill from your office in the seat behind you already thinks you are crazy, not in a funny way, and has spoken with the boss over a 2-cocktail lunch about this and other things. *What other things?* A moment of panic has you gripping the door, jostling it the wrong way, violently, until the flight attendant instructs, *other way, honey.* You take your seat, fasten the seatbelt like a regular belt. You look out the window and are surprised to see a small balloon with a note attached wafting ever upward, and though you know this is impossible—only abstract things like love or god or thin clouds like the mustaches of French movie stars reach these heights—you look away so as not to confirm your suspicions. Later, you call your lover from the hotel room to complain about the flight, the dinner of arrogant slop thrust artlessly before you by a waitress content to barely meet basic needs and move on with it. He doesn't pick up. You finger the fake flower arrangement absently, slip into bed because although Rilke mentioned that we have no reason to mistrust our world, for it is not against us, you do feel a certain pride of ownership over the word *terror*, being like *terroir*, as you have come to represent your homeland of falling asleep, of rolling over to face the wall, of not even wondering in your final conscious moments what a note attached to a balloon at 36,000 feet might say.

FOLDING

We fold under the ennui, the mute spiritus
languishing in group-speak. We fold

the muttered hymns into loops behind
pop songs that we are advised to feel.

We fold across the shuddering
plains of our nation disabused of its raising.

We fold the girl into a woman, fold
the jubilant field into a Big Lot, our shitty cars

parked interminably We fold the quilts—
their warmth unabiding, this strict

decision for a stalwart cool. We fold the animals
into our mouth, for if they are to rest

they must rest entirely. We fold, exhausted,
the white men into abandoned mills—the folds of cloth

they once produced, this infinite industry of garment,
this covering up & turning away.

We fold, terribly weak, into thinking traffic
sounds like the dull monogamy of the ocean

where we were happy once—we fold into the delusion
of similarity that by folding we can replicate

a variety of worship. That god is within us
& with each lover we fold over the same lover

pleated & ruched & gathered at the sides,
is him.

COUNTING THOUGHTS

You know it snowed, for there is snow on the ground, but you don't know when you stopped loving the metal pail of cinders propped against the shed sills, or the way a woman's breast looks from the side when she is sitting on a bed, cradling her face in her hands, or that story about the mailman who filched a young woman's postcards to her Grandmother because there was a certain graceful formality to them. In the olden days, you had 8 chances: train-riding, trench-digging, embroidery, feeling along the ridges of the scalp, slaughtering animals, making shoes or boats. You were born into one or another, depending on the way your father lifted, or did not lift, a shovel over his shoulder, your mother's thumbs pocked with tiny scabs, or licked and wiping crumbs from your cheek. Train wailing through Gdansk at 23:06, you were born, logs lashed together and pushed from the escarpment into the grey and independent sea, you were born. Now you are born into the violent dream of the mocking peak, abandoned oxygen tanks, a frozen hand stretching out of the drift you must hurry past, believing you are chosen. You know you made it this far, for you can see the knee-deep jabs your boots made in the rime trailing behind you, but you do not know when you are permitted to turn back, build a modest fire, take a spot of wine and ask to be taken care of. You know you love, for what else can you call it, but you don't know when you began to address it: your side of the bed, your pile of books on the table, first car you wave down after an accident, or when to stop. How you are so happy to live in the North. The way a slant of sun on the workbench once enacted your labors, not wonderment. Or when to stop. Or when to finally stop. Back then, the slaughtered animals might've heard a solemn chorus of gratitude from around the dinner table. How you weren't born knowing to say Thanks, and furthermore, how it was never your thoughts they counted.

NORTHERN FADO II

I heard a sound.
Top of the rubbish bin sliding
off. I thought of your face—

the particulars that make
the world go
hotter. Your hands

and the mink in them.
Foraging the roadside.

Threw away the Planetarium,
the juice box, ice tray,
Community Center, several
heirloom seeds.

Pressed the can until
the hiss misted out.
Chucked it empty, still unbeautiful.

You were the line
my pillowcase swayed
my car followed absolutely

to an assumed conclusion:
Take me down!

Vodka and an advertisement
for vodka I lived in
some nights pretending

the sound of throwing it
all away, just getting
the fuck out—
was a contractual melody
I wrote for environmentalists.

No, no, they said.
Not your controlled birth,
tent-life-obscenity—
not only your reused carton.

If I come back
may I drink from your palm.

UNWRITING A LETTER

Written on a dear day like no other,

which is to say—
              the greyscale may be Aristotelian, in spite of the eye
              scanning the page without infinite subtext:

Received November cabbaging over the garden,
she ate the heavy meats,   went early to bed
loving Turgenev, she fell past his alphabet
              he did not have fathers
but sons, he did not really have,   with her,
nothing   but the largest letter in the smallest envelope.

Offers were made:

Plastic sheet the garden bed
              she did not soil nor cut back
the rose bush.   Written in a landscape
of ordinary defilement,   a telephone pole
              at the base of his driveway
                first-person-present.

I would like to do this:

Cote d'Ivoire, ransack, possess the exotic privately.

                   Flash the teeth,   to some a smile,

          others sneer.   To have her second

as in after the wealth of bloom and harvest,

a petal pressed between two pages of the night's dark book

to remove her,   allow her to pink a room's encroaching dusk,

          to crush her in his palm.

                 To have her second—

as in the instant before she gives herself away

jumps out of the birthday cake or emerges

          from the suitcase hidden in the shed—when

everything changes including the light   including

          the light of his predicament   known—

first-person-past, reflected as her face in the knife blade

          or the eye of the assailant.

Changing his mind, best not to discuss dreams they are sexless,

          boring, Azaleaed like: *I want to be your brother*

          he imagines   she says   he writes:

                 No, my father.

The meeting will have to be canceled indefinitely:

Outrage of the snow smothering the Zinnias, outrage
of the Mums that cannot go the distance,　　　FTW, the story
of his family　　　he built to love him　　　not her
　　　landscape of pederasty outraged the shut down
town,　　　the absence of alleyways　　　or darkened bars.
Loving to share wine from the plastic cup,　　　outrage at the death
　　　of the plastic cup crushed in his hand like a petal:
Just put her mind to use!　　　That image of her body
in her mind,　　　he wrote,　　　predictably:
　　　I'M SORRY FOR YOUR FEELINGS,　　the you of self-address.

Furthermore, there has been a grave misunderstanding:

I + I + I,　　　　　first-person-plural,　　　church steeples stipple
the valley, she prayed to all of the men he didn't write:
The Queen Anne's Lace autumnal death clench, the insurmountable
white drift in the yard,　beaten-in shape of a body in snow.
　　　He writes: SHE LAY THERE, the weather mounting, pressure
from low to high　　　to finally saying it, relieved epiglottis
　　　the throat's wavering windsock,　　　they, they, it, he—
she lay there with them all.　　　They turned their backs shamelessly.
It was cold, it was beginning to snow, he thought to write but thought

better of it. *I need to, want to move on.* She knew,   threw
it into the fire to warm him up. Rasp,   ash-flutter,   most naked stalk—

Sincerely,   no, with deepest sincerity—*what letter?* her reply:

THIS LANDSCAPE OF CONJUGAL BED

Ghost-haven sheets whiting the soft pond where you lie. You're talking about the dead, the way you can feel them as a shiver of ants across your husband's picnicked body, same-same tan crumbs like sand at an ocean you visited once, brushed from the back of your knee before entering the car. You're talking about the dead, the way you lie down in the same position every night, blink out into separate landscapes, return with an arm thrown across your face, shielding. Against the violence you make the violence; for every man in a trench coat rubbing his hands together on the outskirts of a park, you become blind and shuffle past. You're talking to the dead, you're saying: *It was a good day*. You're saying: *The kids never eat the lunch I pack*. The dead is strikingly aloof, comforting stump smothered in snow. You sit down next to the dead. You want it the old way: Impetuous, stirring all the livelong, drawing you in as a fragile leaf into a gutter. Damn the dead conjured astride each parallel twilight. I love you. I love you. Goodnight.

NOTES

Page 6: *Man's feelings are always purest and most glowing in the hour of greeting and of farewell* is a quote from Jean Paul Richter.

The following quotations:
A life alone makes the need for external demonstration almost disappear (p. 8);
The most likely explanation is that the trouble lies within you (p. 8); and
No man can hope to be completely free who lingers within reach of familiar habits and urgencies (p. 88)
are from Admiral Richard E. Byrd's memoir, *Alone*.

Page 14: The line *The guy who got famous for writing that girls very long ago were innocent, & sad because they were innocent, & beautiful because they were sad, is dead* refers to Hayden Carruth's poem "The Cows at Night."

Page 17: *Let summer come with its schoolboy trumpets and fountains,* and *I cannot think of grass without imagining how it goes yellow secretly, and at the root,* are informed by Donald Justice's poem "Psalm and Lament."

Page 29: *eyes hugged by lids unpainted, not resembling the blue hue reminiscent of orgasm, the flood of blood to the lips, the nag of the lengthening neck* refers to the historical use of makeup to mimic sexual arousal. Worldwide expenditures for cosmetics hover around $19 billion annually.

Page 35: Shirley Horn (1934–2005) was a master pianist, jazz vocalist, and, for some years, a full-time office worker.

Page 37: *Vollmann's myopic account bearing the loveliness of sludge weighting the Black Robes's hem* refers to the Jesuits in William Vollmann's book *Fathers and Crows*.

Page 41: Beardman Jugs, sometimes called Bellermine Jugs, are stoneware featuring a bearded face, sometimes malevolent, found on many shipwrecked Dutch vessels of the 17th century.

Page 52: Robert Peary (1856–1920) was a U.S. explorer who claimed, April 6, 1909, to have reached the Geographic North Pole, a claim oft disputed. Peary made many expeditions to the Arctic, and famously brought several Inuit to the U.S. where, lacking immunity, most died. Minik Wallace, whose life is chronicled in *Give Me My Father's Body*, was among them. Peary also took several meteorites, the Inuit's only source of iron.

Page 55: The lines *how hard it is to tell | who's gonna love you the best* come from Karen Dalton's song "In the Evening." This poem is for Steffen Brown.

Page 92: The title "Numbers are Many, Words are Limited" was lifted from the final lines in Chapter Five of Lao Tzu's *Dao De Jing*, translated by Christopher Kiely.

Page 95: "The End of Nature" contains references to two quotes by Rilke. The first: *"The point of marriage is not to create a quick commonality by tearing down all boundaries; on the contrary, a good marriage is one in which each partner appoints the other to be the guardian of his solitude, and thus they show each other the greatest possible trust. A merging of two people is an impossibility, and where it seems to exist, it is a hemming-in, a mutual consent that robs one party or both parties of their fullest freedom and development. But once the realization is accepted that even between the closest people infinite distances exist, a marvelous living side-by-side can grow up for them, if they succeed in loving the expanse between them, which gives them the possibility of always seeing each other as a whole and before an immense sky."* The second: *"For beauty is nothing but the beginning of terror which we are barely able to endure, and it amazes us so, because it serenely disdains to destroy us."*

ABOUT THE AUTHOR

PAIGE ACKERSON-KIELY is the author of *In No One's Land*, winner of the 2006 Sawtooth Poetry Prize, selected by D.A. Powell, and other works of poetry and prose. She lives in rural Vermont, co-edits *A Handsome Journal*, and works at a homeless shelter.

AHSAHTA PRESS

SAWTOOTH POETRY PRIZE SERIES

2002: Aaron McCollough, *Welkin* (Brenda Hillman, judge)

2003: Graham Foust, *Leave the Room to Itself* (Joe Wenderoth, judge)

2004: Noah Eli Gordon, *The Area of Sound Called the Subtone* (Claudia Rankine, judge)

2005: Karla Kelsey, *Knowledge, Forms, The Aviary* (Carolyn Forché, judge)

2006: Paige Ackerson-Kiely, *In No One's Land* (D. A. Powell, judge)

2007: Rusty Morrison, *the true keeps calm biding its story* (Peter Gizzi, judge)

2008: Barbara Maloutas, *the whole Marie* (C. D. Wright, judge)

2009: Julie Carr, *100 Notes on Violence* (Rae Armantrout, judge)

2010: James Meetze, *Dayglo* (Terrance Hayes, judge)

2011: Karen Rigby, *Chinoiserie* (Paul Hoover, judge)